ROUTE
TO
DESTRUCTION

ROUTE
TO
DESTRUCTION

A Collection of Poetry
and Spoken Word

PJ

PHOENIX JAMES

ROUTE TO DESTRUCTION

First Edition: 2022

ISBN: 978-1-7397925-2-7 (Paperback)
ISBN: 978-1-7397925-3-4 (Ebook)

Cover Artwork & Design by Phoenix James.
Book Design & Formatting by Phoenix James.

Visit the author's website at www.PhoenixJamesOfficial.com or email him at phoenix@PhoenixJamesOfficial.com

DEDICATION

To all who lived for me
To all who died for me
To all who fought for me
And to all who fight for me
I hope you find this worthy

To those yet to find the words
I'm pleased this reached you

And to a young boy
Who long ago
Embraced being different
And standing out from the crowd
Suffered the costs
And stood again
And again
And again
You were right

Thank you for dreaming
Thank you for believing
I wouldn't be here without it

I hope I've done a good job
I hope you're smiling a big smile.

CONTENTS

A LAND WHERE MINDS ARE FREE

Absent
From the activities
Of the busy city
Off the old road
Through the forest
Over the mountains
And across the sea
There's a land
Where minds are free
I know because I have been
I know because I have seen
The flow of realised dreams
As fluent as rivers and streams
A place where man
Fails not to achieve
Where he doubts not
But believes
Staying deeply rooted
In his foundation
As like the trees
Not blowing aimlessly
On the wind
Like its leaves
And I have seen here

No pain
No rain
In any form
No shame
No scorn
Only peace in knowing
The sun shines also on the inside
Where there is no morning
No noon
And no night
Only light
And the height of success
Is not a point to be reached
But merely an ongoing flight
Or quest for man to be his best
Not a fight or plight
But simply a strengthening test
And there is where
I have seen man
Utilise the equations of God
To the point that he knows no fear
Challenged but well balanced
And well prepared
For all of life's circumstances
Amidst life's adversities
His soul dances

He takes chances without limit
For trial and tribulation
Only enhance his spirit
And I know because I have seen
I know because I have been
Absent
From the activities
Of the busy city
Off the old road
Through the forest
Over the mountains
And across the sea
To a land
Where minds are free.

A NEW WAY OF THINKING

It was in the park
After dark
I witnessed the start
Of the glory
A new realisation of self
The missing part
Of the story
A new way of thinking
And a new path
Was before me
A new revelation
And a sign
Sent to restore me
I was held in a trance
By an electromagnetic force field
Which prepared me
For all that life
Was about to reveal
Now I see and feel the things
Other men don't feel and see
But I guess this is the way
That it was supposed to be
Now close to me
The candle light

Burns bright as I write
It's quiet
It's just past midnight
And the only time
Things have ever felt this right
Me and the night are alike
We bring the sunlight
New days
New ways
New beginnings
New ways of doing things
Doesn't matter when the bell rings
It's not over
Until we sing
A new way of thinking
Minds are linking
This is what it's about
We've got to do this now
We've got no choice
Time is running out
Somehow
We've got to find a way out
Now
Or stay here and die
But no way
Not I

No way
I'm alive
Look at me
I can fly
Way up high in the sky
I'll survive
I was made for this
Pressurised
And now with open eyes
I can see us
Like caged birds
Still singing
Calling for something
Or someone else to free us
But it can't be
Can't we see?
We're already free
Because only really the soul
Has destiny
To me
It's a new degree of possibility
It's a new way to be
It's a new way of thinking
To stop our ship sinking
Amidst the destruction
And disaster

Prevailing
Creating a plain sailing
For those in the hereafter
Life
And I've taken control of my soul
So it never dies
As I reside
In the presence
And company of the wise
I become excellence
Personified
And no longer shall I have to hide
From what's inside
I realise
My pride
Will only eat me alive
So I rise
Rise
Rise
Rise
With a new way of thinking
And a new way of thought
Only to find
My piece of mind
Just can't be bought
Or sold

Too specially designed
Worth more than gold
Now only the physical grows old
As I behold
The spiritual manifestation
From all the revelation
I was told
And you know
It was elevation for my soul
Elevation
For my soul
Elevation
For my soul
Elevation
For my soul.

A TASTE OF DEATH

The vampires are on the attack
They come in the form of men
And in the form of bats
Ready to drink my blood
But I ain't giving up
The vultures are above
Circling overhead
Waiting for my weakest moment
Closest to being dead
So they can descend upon me
And eat up my flesh
I say a prayer for the best
Though the stress
Has got me heavily breathing
North
South
East
And West
I'm surrounded by demons
Possessed beings
After my semen
Want to see me die bleeding
From being skinned alive
Still I survive their attempted beating

And their lies
Told only so they can see my demise
They're trying to stick a stake
Through my heart
Chasing me towards the graveyard
With their poison darts
And poison hearts
The hyenas just look on and laugh
As if to say
He's a dead man he won't last
I'm scared
But I won't let fear get the better half
I'm prepared for war
But I'm running fast
For this day
I see conniving
Malicious bitches
Turn into the witches that they really are
Petrifying
With a life full of scars
They're on me
Haunting me like ghosts and zombies
I never did anything wrong
But they want me gone
So anxious to see my end
I'm surrounded like Daniel

In the lions den
Never again
Will I call you friends
You who me to my death you send
Envious
Jealous women and men
Maniacs and suicidals
Want to take my life
On the same downward spiral
Want to nail me to the cross
Like Christ was in the bible
Crucified
So you can continue to worship
Graven images and idols
You hypocrites and parasites
Whom to which my death is vital
May you behold
And witness the wrath of this recital
And just as I escaped
The fiery lake
And two anacondas
Ready to crush my bones
I'm faced with the grim reaper
And about fifty dim sleepers
I'm contemplating taking out on my own
Then at that moment

A dozen flaming arrows are thrown
I duck
And luckily I make it home
By employing all tactics
Created a decoy
And then hid in the attic
Where I met poison spiders
But the fact is
I'm just too acrobatic
Made it to the roof
Through the skylight
Still bleeding from being mobbed
Still pleading with God
For my life
Onto the street again
On my feet again
Where I meet again
Vampires are on the attack
They come in the form of men
And in the form of bats
Ready to drink my blood
But I ain't giving up
The vultures are above
Circling overhead
Waiting for my weakest moment
Closest to being dead

So they can descend upon me
And eat up my flesh
But despite all they have tried
And all they have said
This has only served
And demonstrated as a test
For I
Have already died
My first death
I have risen.

ABORT

We as man
Have become the robots
And the androids
We long sought to create
To aid and to serve us
We exist now
Only to maintain and improve
On the technological systems
Machinery and electronics
We've caused to exist
We are all now
The maintenance workers
And systems operators of them
We've taught them all we know
And enabled them
To become faster than us
And smarter than us
To even think for us
And in the process
Have allowed ourselves
To become docile and dumb
We mighty
Masterful
Majestic

Magnificent men
Once upon a time
Are now merely mechanical
Who now know only of the mechanics
Of the mechanisms we've made
Mightier than ourselves
Which now own us
And are the owners of our minds
See what we have become
Minute and minuscule
Microcosms
Of our former magnitude
Now consumed
In the wizardry of circuitry
And ruled
By our own embellished
And fancified yet perishable
And destructive
Ill-formed finery
It is we that are at fault
We've come to naturally worship
The functionality
Of man made accessories
More than nature
And mankind itself
And the human functioning people

We once functioned as
We've fashioned ourselves
Into superficial cyborgs
Dependant on silicon
And cellular communication
Our now neglected
Ill-treated
Broken down
Corrupted
Fried up
Malfunctioned
And fragmented faculties fail us
We've transformed ourselves
Into mentally manipulated mules
Driven by our own foolery
And so
The once wise
We now arrive as fools
Downgraded
But updated
To the latest upgrade
So now we're disguised as cool
Redefined
But no longer designed
To concentrate in school
Or learn at the rate that we used to

We've high priced gadgets
And lowered IQs
We've traded in our minds
For more time
Our knowledge for technology
So of course
At the flick of a switch
The touch of a finger tip
Everything appears
To be working properly
Where was I
We've given all of our memory
And smartness
To these gadgets and devices
It is we
That are now dependant on them
For our speed
Functionality
Knowledge
And intelligence
We are now merely
The aids and servants of them
Slaves to them
Moving forward and backward
Only under their supervision
Assisting their system

And working only to serve
And improve them
All in order to have a life
All in order for us to live
Or to feel alive

If you are still there
And you can still think
For yourself
Without the aid of them
Please
Before it's too late
Abort.

ACTS FOR CHANGE

You may feel
That your current circumstances
Are not right for you
To move forward
Or to succeed at this time
That your present situation
And environment
Is not set up in the right way
For you to fully
And confidently take action
For your thing to begin
For it to work for you
Or for you to progress
Beyond where you are right now
Or for your change to come
Take massive enormous action
Right where you are right now
In the small space
You currently occupy
And with the limited resources
You have at your disposal
Do not wait
To get a changed situation
And environment to act

Get a change in your situation
And environment
By getting into action
Things only change
When we act
On changing things.

BEWARE

We haven't got much time
So this must be brief
You are the chosen
Therefore you must know
The visions I see
I see our planet earth
On route to destruction
World leaders
Playing their part in its disruption
By means of controlled corruption
Behind great warfares
I see pre-constructions
Cut downs in human production
Food contamination
For human consumption
Alteration
Of the body's spiritual ability to function
By the mind isolation
Persuasion
Re-education of societies
Based on lies and secrecies
With objectives
Only to achieve supremacy
I see cover-ups

And transactions
More than enough
To keep a man hush-hush
From telling us
The truth
They bluff
So who can we trust
They're watching us now too
So let's move
Just keep walking
I'll do the talking
There's a lot you don't know yet
A lot you won't get
And a lot you're not supposed to
Just keep walking
And I'll show you
You see
In the beginning
It's not what you're thinking
Things didn't exactly happen
In the Garden of Eden
The way we've been believing
In fact
We're descendants
From celestial beings
We've just been

Prevented from seeing
Now all this information
Can be traumatising
Especially with the thought
Of our hard task ahead
And slim chance of surviving
But we still can
With this information
You must devise a plan
You may not see me again
Because they know who I am
Here, take this
It's an Ankh
A very powerful amulet
Wear it around your neck
And don't forget
Now it won't make you respected
But it'll keep you protected
Against the matrix
Now, take this
Inside it contains
All the info you need to know
Everything they don't want us to see
Everything from extraterrestrials
To a wealth of conspiracy
Use them wisely

And set our people free
Time is running out
I must leave you now
But keep an eye out
And don't forget
Be aware of what's going on
In the streets
And on your TV set
Here, now watch these movies
But remember
They're only half the truth
The other half
Is only there
To keep you confused
Go safely.

BLOODSTAINED CONCRETE

As this
Bloodstained concrete
Beneath my feet
Speaks yet another volume
Of more death in the street
It tells of more police meeting
And maintaining agendas
Of another mission complete
By keeping more drug dealers
In business
Even if this is
Only for a time at least
It speaks of gun crime on the increase
And of mums finding no peace
From crying without cease
From seeing their young ones
Dying in the streets
Sometimes it sings when it speaks
Sad songs
Of all the wrongs
And all the grief
Come stand with me
Upon this haunting ground
In this taunting place

And hear the cries
Of this once ordinary grey pave
That now wears a bloodstained face
As it tells the in-depth stories
Of murder
Brutality
And violation
Inflicted on innocent victims
In countless police stations
It says the same blood
Running across the floor in there
Is the same blood you see
Staining my face out here
Its cold voice
Cuts through me
Raw and authoritative
Speaking
Of corrupt law enforcement officers
And fraudulent governments
Who ship in and fly in weapons
And drugs
As if mental enslavement isn't enough
Without blood on the pavement
Distributing them
Throughout our communities
Adding further fuel

To our death
Decline
And disunity
Hurting
While they just sit back
And watch us destroy each other
Discuss how good it's working
Then order their wicked workmen
Their crooked coppers
To arrest
And try and pocket the profits off of us
In this grandiose design
Designed to meet a grandiose purpose
Black blood
Continues to spill out into the streets
Because in the laws grand scheme of things
It's worthless
Too late for doctors and nurses
Cries this
Here cold concrete
As it continues to record these injustices
Upon its surface
Word is
You might die here
On what the local papers call Murder mile
But don't be discouraged

Come stand with me a while
Upon this haunting ground
In this taunting place
Where the pavement stays shiny red
From the common blood on its face
Yes, shiny red
With more shine
Than hair designed
With products by Nexxus
More glistening
Than a Gucci diamond necklace
Runs smoother and faster
Than a brand new Lexus
And draws more attention
Than a girl group from Texas
Yes
Come stand with me
And hear these tainted streets cry freedom
Freedom from the blood of those bleeding
But there comes no relief
From the guns and drugs they keep feeding
Into our communities
Destroying our belief
In love and unity
With so much evil in our neighbourhood
It's difficult to see any good

Then we wonder why
Our youngsters
Don't behave as they should
It's all
In the mind
Control
System
Of thieves
Don't take my brain away
Need to think
Or soon we'll be
Extinct
By this strategically
Manufactured disease
Mass genocide is taking place
Outside
And on our TVs
Right before our eyes
And still millions of closed minds
Can't see
That this is all by design
And meant to be
Mentally
Physically
And spiritually
It's deep

There goes another soul put to sleep
Through drugs
And gun crime on the increase
Everyday it's the same old repeat
And as this cold wind
Blows through me
I stand here listening
To the testimonies
Of this
Bloodstained concrete
Beneath my feet
Speaking
Yet another volume
Of more death
In the street.

CROOKED SYSTEM

In the space of six and a half hours
He came back
With three mobile phones
A TV
A laptop
And a car stereo
I was like...

He was like
We will survive
This system
Ain't designed for us, bro
I said, but don't the minimum wage
Pay enough for us
To get through these rainy days
Doesn't society
Create enough legitimate ways
For us to get paid
Without stealing

He said, nope
Not without feeling like robotic slaves
Which only leads to serious stress
Or rebellion

From constantly
And unhappily working 9-5
Just to stay alive
Some say it's no surprise
We turn to street crime

I said, but isn't the system
Designed for us to achieve
Aren't there enough institutions
Funded for us
To be all we can be
Enough developmental establishments
Designed to nurture
And channel our creativity

He said, no
Which is why
All our beautiful talents
Become and remain suppressed
Rather than encouraged
And expressed
Bottled up like a fizzy drink
Just waiting to burst
Some say
To create the solution
Observe the problem first

Or in no time at all
It just gets worse

In this case, I said
Another chain
Another handbag
Another purse

Exactly, he said
Another car stereo
Another video
TV
DVD
Another laptop
Another life
How long until who can put it right
Gets hurt
Think about it
It works

I said, but aren't there already
Enough outlets
Facilities
Programmes and schemes
To occupy the mind
Of the enquiring youth today

Isn't it equal opportunities
For both woman and man
Can't we get the same jobs
And same wages others can
Or is it
That our plan of progress
Is doomed
Even before we've began

He said, that's right, my man
Now you're beginning to understand.

DECLARATION OF EMANCIPATION

I no longer care
For their opinions
I respectfully decline
From listening
I have understanding
Enough
To rely
On my own wisdom
I take all responsibility
For my own decisions
I am the pilot
And captain
Of my mission
I create the system
I design my own curriculum
I dictate the rhythm
I hold dominion
Over my own position
I own the life I'm living
I define my own existence.

DESIRE TO BE FREE

Sometimes
I can't help but wonder
What the outcome will be
Of this continuous
Uphill struggle for life
This burning
Heartfelt desire
To be free
I write these
Not fully knowing
What the future will hold
But still with the belief
That I can save my soul
And if I should save not my own
But save yours in turn
Weep not
For the blessings and rewards
Of the same
Have been earned
It's my concern
That you should make it
Through the crisis
And not be lost
To the destruction

Of mankind's devices
Like the so many who died
Before knowing what life is
For we are as one
And share the same likeness
Time has come now
For me to recite this
So you may hear
And fully receive Phenzwaan
Bringer of the light
With new life in my palm
With me you will see no harm
Only the best
After the storm there's a calm
This is just a test
And I must confess
I've been weak at times
But together we are strength
If we unite minds
I feel you
And my plan is that you should too
Feel me
For apart we only waver
But together
We are free
To move in any direction

Reach any destination or degree
I'm told I was sent to lead
And I do believe
So please
In these turbulent seasons
And times
Come take a walk
Through my mind
Seek and you shall find
And see a revolution for mankind
My kind
Our kind
See and feel the signs
Which reveal the rhyme
And the reasons behind
Because the coins of destiny
Shine both sides at a time
Which makes fate
Something we create
And something we decide
This ocean is wide
But I can't hide from you
It would be foolish to try
Let this ship sink
And we both die
For I am your future

As you are mine
What affects me
Indirectly affects you
This I can't deny
In you too lie
The powers to fly
To fly
To fly
So carry on you strong one
Carry on
Carry on
Carry on
For your job is not yet done
The battle is not yet won
It's only just begun
Neglect not your daughters
And your sons
Into negative temptation
It only leads to mental starvation
And non elevation for our nation
Take your station
And defend your soul
Against these evil killing fields
Some men are bold
But cling to heels
Of those who can't help them

First seek your own path
And become your own friend
Because to follow such men
Only leads to mayhem
And lose ends
Find yourself and grow
Maintain mind
Health
Body and soul
Because sometimes
You just never know
What the outcome will be
Of this continuous
Uphill struggle for life
This burning
Heartfelt desire
To be free.

EARLSWOOD

You know
They say
What you become in life
Isn't stamped
On your birth certificate
Some of us were adopted
And expected just to live with it
Not knowing who
Or where our real parents were
Or if they were even still alive
Some of us were ex-prisoners
And couldn't cope with the difference
Of life on the outside
Some of us
Didn't know how
To deal with the death
Or absence of a loved one
So a part of us died
Some of us
Simply couldn't deal with being alone
And it's said that the sickness
Was caused for example
By a sibling leaving home
Some of us were rape victims

Some of us were filled with anger
And hate for governmental systems
Some of us were forced into marriage
Forced to bear the baggage
Of something we couldn't manage
Some of us were alcohol abusers
As a result from relationships
That you could call
Abusive
Some of us couldn't handle the pressure
Of being in gangs
Others of us couldn't handle the pressure
Of completing exams
Some of us were prisoners of war
Some of us were homeless
And sleeping on floors
Some of us were sexually abused
And became sexually abusive
Some of us were in serous debt
From bad investments
And became reclusive
They often concluded
That some parents paid
For their children's care
To use the asylum
As a dumping ground

For unwanted relatives
Rather than an experimental alternative
To care at home
They said the burden of care
Fell mostly on women
That is, on mothers
Daughters
And sisters
Of the disabled
Or old
That institutionalisation
May well have followed
A particular 'crisis of caring'
Within the household
They said, we all revealed the diversity
Of the insane population
In Victorian England
And that we were among those
Deemed unsuitable
For immediate release
Into the community
They said, they were too preoccupied
With managing violent
And dangerous defectives
Or with ensuring the treatment
Of the 'curable cases' among us

And that there was little time
Or money
To consider the appropriate care
Of chronic
Harmless
Incurable patients
From the outside
For the many that passed that way
In the carriages on their journeys
From Horley to Redhill and back again
It was a glimpse
Of a fine Victorian architectural dream
Of perfectibility
For many of us
The inmates
The ones on the inside
Under concentration
It became a terrible
Terrible nightmare
Of life-long segregation.

ELEVATE

How can we elevate
Let's get together
Let's talk
Why wait
How can we elevate
I want to know how
Before it gets too late
And why do we always
Contemplate fate
Instead of concentrate
On ways to be great
I want to know now
What changes we can make
And how long it will take
To elevate our minds
And find more positive states
In order to make changes
And deal with the issues we face
I can come to your house
Or you can come to my place
Or anywhere where
We can further discuss this case
I feel that we are both
Trying to get somewhere

And that our destinations
May even be the same
Well if this is so
Then any time spent together
Will not go in vain
But only serve
To ease the strain of any pain
Our journey may contain
Lets get together and exchange
Numbers and names
So we can arrange
To meet and discuss
The concerns at hand
So we can sit down together
And devise a plan
Because after
Every individual's situation
There should be
A learnt lesson
And but one question at stake
How can I
Elevate.

FLOWERS

I wish
You could've heard
And seen
How much we love you
Instead of the unspoken words
We were all keeping from you
What good are all the accolades
And praise to you now
All the things we didn't say
When you were around
All of the pent up ego and pride
Really burns after the fact
And can't be good for our health
That and knowing
The warmth you gave to our hearts
Now only serves ourself
All the quotes and eulogies
Might make us feel better
But won't make it right
That we show we appreciate you
More in your death
Than we did in life
Unfortunately
No one alive can tell us

If you'll get the message
That we loved you more than life
Being as final as death is
We were all well aware
We couldn't turn back the times
Yet we wait until its too late
To share with you what's on our minds
We wait until you're late
To tell you how great you are
On stage telling the audience
But never told the star
We're recalling your stories
And applauding you
Now you're long gone
After we remained silent
Watching you during your swan song
We saw you sailing away like we all will
And whispered so long
Our grand show of appreciation
Gone wrong
If you're watching and listening now
I hope you find it in you to forgive us
The backward
Selfish
Inconsiderate
Careless

Stream of consciousness that is us
How we value the dead in death
And not the living while they're alive
Will always be with us
The inner shame and self torment
Of knowing the love we had for you
We didn't show enough
Now your days here are gone
And we carry on
And carry the burden
Of what we've done and always do
Miss what we had when it's gone
After withholding our adoration
And all the praise that was due
We seemingly dismiss the thought
That the people we admire
Won't always be there
Let's give the people we love
The chance to see
Feel
And smell
All their flowers
While they're still here.

GIVING THANKS

I'm head over heels
In love with you
Nothing comes above
The things you do
The things you say
Brighten up my world
You mean more to me
Than money
Diamonds and pearls
The wondrous things
You bring forth
Make my soul pleased
More than cuisine
Or Caribbean seas
I'd cruise the world
To make you all right
To see you happy
Is my delight
Let nothing come between
The oneness we have
Let nothing soil our goodness
And make it bad
It's immeasurable
To say the least

The heights
You make me reach
It's impossible
To define them
In a single speech
You take me
Way above the high rises
And condominiums
Of the street
You lift my entire spirit
And make it complete
You're in a class of your own
That many aspire to surpass
But against your consistency
They just wouldn't last
I've travelled many miles
Alone with you
Just to hear your conversation
And behold
The qualities you posses
Could exalteth a nation
You preserve and restore me
In my times of need
Like the sun and the rain
Preserve and restore the seed
The sum

Of a thousand pounds a day
Just couldn't suffice
The exceeding joy
You bring to my life
The exceptional pleasure
That comes from your presence
Is very much unlike many
The essence
Of your entire composition
Would indeed make good
For any
No matter what the situation
You're always there at my side
You reveal my truest thoughts
And I could never hide
The expressive nature
You bring out in me
You show me all my life is
And all it can be
You are your own
And I've truly encountered
None like you
You're wondrous
And nothing compares
To the things you do
I give thanks.

I WRITE

I said it before
So I'm only going to say it once
I write
For those born on the first
Second
Third
And fourth day of the month
I write for monks
And Christians
Nuns
And Hare Krishnas
Those who carry guns
And ammunition
All governmental systems
Arabians
Muslims
And ancient Egyptians
I write for all those in life
Desiring higher positions
I write for the man on a mission
And the independent woman
Making her own decisions
I write for Buddhists
Jews

And Rastafarians
Hindus
Vegans
Meat eaters
And vegetarians
I write for lawyers
And librarians
Historians
Taureans
And Aquarians
Sagittarians
And all the others
I write for baby mothers
And baby fathers
Barbers
I write for the fishmongers
Down at the Barbados harbours
For the governments
Trying to starve us
Or retard us
From feeding us garbage
I write for nurses
And doctors
Surgeons
Pilots in planes
And helicopters

Hip-hoppers
Gatecrashers
And show stoppers
Police
And traffic blockers
Menders
Street vendors on street corners
Coroners
And mourners
I write for crackheads
And kids on mopeds
Divorcees
And newlyweds
Widows
And weed heads
I write for the dead
I write for presidents of countries
Asses
And monkeys
Junk food junkies
Girls that dumped me
And the mob that once jumped me
I write for rapists
And serial killers
Ex-cons
And escaped prisoners

I write for forgiveness
I write pain
Because I live this
I write with vividness
To create vivid pictures
With vivid images
I write for infidelity
And religiousness
Believers
And atheists
I write for the craziest
And the laziest
I write for geologists
And ufologists
All scientists
In all sciences
In all fields
I write for big deals
So I can eat comfortably
And not have to steal
I write what I feel
Hardly fictitious
When it's all
Real
It's what knowledge is
I write for theologists

And fools
Colleges
And schools
Tutors
And students
Unions
And movements
I write for health
And institutions
Of self-improvement
I write for newborn babies
Men in uniform
And scorned old ladies
I write for queens
And kings
A drunkard
And two tramps
Going through rubbish bins
Natives
And foreigners
Old war heroes
And warriors
Emergency services
And couriers
Beggars
And borrowers

Campaign leaders
And followers
I write for United Nations
Illegal organisations
Miseducation
And my own denomination
Among the commuters
Of a packed out train station
I write for the man
Who tills the plantation
I write for aggravation
And lack of patience
I write for maniacs
And psychos
With no diagnosed head cases
I write in strange places
Sometimes alone
Sometimes among strange faces
I write for status
And for those who think it's wrong
For me to want to be famous
I write shameless
Not careless or aimless
I write for world peace
I write for rappers
Actors

Singers
And athletes
I write for nightclubbers
And lovers
Sisters
And brothers
My one-night stands
With no rubbers
I write for poetry
And MC
For mic love
And CD
For collection
And PC
For music
And movie
For dub
And publicity
For love
And unity
I write for you
I write for me
So hopefully
We can see now
That the hand that writes
Is as good as the hand

That holds
The plough.

IN KNOWING YOURSELF

Finding yourself
Is a never-ending
Ongoing journey
Our self discovery
Is forever in motion
The world we exist in
Is ever-changing
The energy
Of the consistently
Expanding universe
We draw ourselves from
Is never still
The planet
And everything on
Around
And within it
Is constantly shifting
Knowledge of self therefore
Is not a point to be reached
It is an arrival
At one destination
From another
While on route to the next
There's always more to teach

There's always more to learn
There's always room to grow
And there's forever more to know
Nothing alive stays the same
We are never in the same space
Same way
Same place
Evolve
Evolve more
Then evolve again
Repeat.

JIMMY'S GOT A LOADED GUN

Shots fired
Jimmy's got a loaded gun
What were you thinking
How do you intend
To evacuate
An already abandoned building
Filled with children
Already dead inside
Void of light
Self destructing
Self employed
Victims of the night
Self deprecating
Selfish and selfless
The ones they avoid
Seek, kill and destroy
You're helpless
How can you help us
We
Just want to set all of our hostages free
Offends us
Your lack of belief
There goes
Another unanswered ransom note

Please
What can you offer us
Just leave us be
All of this time wasting is costing us
If I was you
Then I would see
No
I would rather be me
It looks safer on this side
Jimmy's got a loaded gun
Had it on layaway
Smiled
Counting down the days
While you were
Spouting all the things you say
Paid up on payday
It's wild how things change
Vowed he won't live a slave
The night we all prayed
Something about
The wages of thy ways
Won't go unpaid
We couldn't all be saved
But we can be safe
You had a role to play
You were out of place

Now Jimmy's got a loaded gun
And another one
Just in case.

KEEP GOING

In pursuing your goals
Dreams
Desires
And ambitions
Be prepared to go further
Than you think you should have to go
Keep going
Be prepared to go that added distance
And extra few miles
Go further
Than you thought you ever could
Keep going
Go further than you have the energy
Strength
Perseverance
Resilience
Patience
And willpower for
Keep going
And then
Go some more
Be ready
To run into rejection
And ridicule on your path

And people who will let you down
Underestimate you
Undermine you
Sidestep you
Overlook you
And take you for granted
You can be sure
That there will be those
Along the way
Who will oppose
What you are trying to achieve
And where you are aiming to go
Keep going
Those who will put you down
And try to contaminate your mind
With their negative viewpoints
And narrow thinking
Do not stop at this point
Many do
Keep going
Keep moving in the direction of progress
There are those too
Who will smile with you
And say go for it
But want nothing more
Than to see you fail

While placing obstacles in your way
Never mind
You will recognise them
Just keep going
Along the way
You will also
Have some of the most uplifting
And surreal experiences
Witness some truly beautiful things
And meet some very special people
Who will all have
An amazing impact
On your life
And who you are as a person
You will recognise these people also
They will inspire you to keep going
Keep them close to you
Along with the things that motivate you
Inspire you
And make you feel good
And positive about yourself
And your journey
If at any time you happen to fall down
Along the way
Simply get back up
Dust yourself off

Get back on your horse
And carry on going
When the way turns dark
And you feel helpless
And there's no one around
To show you the way
Or to tell you
If you're heading in the right direction
And you feel like quitting
And turning back
Keep going
It's all about progression
Meaningful progress
Towards the attainment
Of a worthwhile goal
Is very seldom an easy ride
When you're ready to give in
Keep going
When you're ready to give up
Keep going
When you're ready to give out
Keep going
Don't question why
Or how long for
The beauty
The treasure

And the magic
Is all in the journey
You will see
Just keep going
Keep going
And keep going.

LAST CHANCE

I am writing this
For you
So you may understand
The reason why I'm here
And just the kind of man I am
I have a very important purpose here
And one that I must fulfil
For if I don't
Many will suffer
At the hands of evil
And some will even be killed
There are many of us
Who have been sent here
To carry out this gracious task
If it is not accomplished
Our future generations
Will not come to pass
We've been sent out
On an outreach
To touch Gods people of the earth
To raise them up
From their old ways
Showing them
What life is really worth

Our time now is short
But these duties
Must be carried out
We've been coming here for centuries
But our most crucial time is now
Like soldiers for the battlefield
The wise and appointed
Must be brave
And take their stance
Because time is running out
And there won't be a last chance.

LOST SOUL

As my mind travels
Across the hemisphere
Everything everywhere
Becomes clear
Elder citizens
Cars
Children
And buildings
Are minute from up here
No ground beneath my feet
No ground beneath my Nike Air
Without a care
I've taken flight
Tell my mum
I won't be home tonight
Within the twinkling of an eye
It's as if I've been resurrected
I wonder
Who's going to spend
All that money I collected
And who's going to date
All those girls that I neglected
But when I check it
It was to be expected

I was always the outcast
Always felt rejected
And dissed
I wonder
If Jesus had it like this
I've ascended
And I'm sure to be missed
My life now tells a story
Similar to his
And as yesterday's memories
Become old
I try to keep hold
At all costs
Is God in control
Of my soul
Or is lost.

MAYBE TODAY

Sometimes
We fail to see the light
Maybe today
It'll shine bright
And maybe today
We'll find
Some peace of mind
Because only God knows
How long we've been trying
To see some sun shine
Through
On the things we do
And who's to say
Today
We may see a way through
The troubles and strife
And even though everyday life
Throws another roll of the dice
We learn to play our hand
Even when our cards ain't nice

And we don't quit
Even when our hardest hit
We stick to it

Because you can never tell
How close you are
It may be near
When it seems so far
Remember
Everyone's a shining star
With a capable chemistry to achieve
Anything they want to
If they believe
And I know it's real
So I take it from here
Where I can feel
An energy
Propelling me
Telling me
To put it down for you
And I will too
Because all the things that affect me
Indirectly affect you

It's true
And it's enough to drive you
Round the bend
When you discover
Another ain't really your friend
But still

Let's get up and try again
My friends
We can't let the negatives
Hold us down
No way
Let's pick our dreams up
From off the ground
And be not so easily swayed
By the troubles
And the turmoils of the day
That seem to float through the air
Instead let's ask ourselves the question
Why are we here?
And even though an equal amount
Simply just don't care
Let's be the ones to make a change
And turn things around this year
And next year
Without fear
Knowing where we're going
Let's keep this karma flowing

It's mind blowing
To know that where the mind goes
The body follows
For the mind controls the body

And thoughts control actions
Now
This is only just a fraction
Of my reaction
To a mother earth
In serious contraction
For all I see
Is grief on the streets
In a city where hearts bear no pity
It's far from pretty
And there sure ain't no unity
In my community
I've been seeing this since puberty
And it's a real calamity
It seems as though
We've forsaken all humanity
I see so many lose their sanity
Over vanity
So I pray for our rationality

As I sow these seeds
And plead
That they won't fall by the wayside
Because of pride
I look at men's lives
And feel uninspired

Because all I see
Is pain inside
And fear in their eyes
I think it's about time we rise
And be extra careful
Not to get roped in
Because it's so easy
To adopt the wrong thing
That's why I sing a song
And try to build a strong team
With a positive theme
So a positive future
Can be seen
Here's hoping
We all achieve our dreams
And my spirit is unrelenting
This is a manifestation
Of the faith that I was sent in
Which liberates me
From my fears
So let all those that have ears
Hear

Because I see a future
Beyond the darkness
I never used to

Because it was never like this
It was dull but it's brighter now
I see blue skies
Beyond the rain filled clouds
And yesterday
Did really end last night
Today's a new day
And it looks bright
I think what I'll do
Is take a vacation
And from now on
Look for the benefits
In every situation
No longer being impatient
Just being the best that I can be

And if you see me on the street
Or at the club
Greet me with enthusiasm
And love
Because
Even though
My mentality
Rises up out of the ghetto
I'm still attached to the stem
Just like a rose petal

Hoping one day
I'll be able to pass by the corners
And not see
The brothers hanging out
Doing the same old things
Smoking
And calling at the women
Every time they came about
But simply had a change of heart
And decided to make a new start

You say
But it's hard in this life
And that
I don't deny
But that doesn't grant you the excuse
Not to try
I mean
Tell me why
Do some stall
While others just fly by
Some take a nose dive
Some fly low
And some fly high
Some are even petrified
So bless those who try

And those who take the time out
To work this rhyme out
Just to find out
What it's all about
Because
Every line counts
That's why I wrote it down

And in the hope
That we should not be like
Lambs to the slaughter
I've led many horses to water
But never been able
To make them drink
Hopefully this one
Will make them think
And begin to look inside themselves
And realise
That there's nothing missing
And that goes for you too
So listen
For as long as the stars glisten
Stay on your mission
And let no soul deter you
From your ambition
It's your decision

To be or not to be
Don't let Mr and Mrs know it all
Control your destiny
And who am I
Phenzwaan
Giving you
The best
In me.

MIND CONTROL

I do hereby declare
And say this
All families
Friends
And neighbours
It's a new order of the ages
And we're all on the front pages
Of major changes
Now some claim this
Statement as outrageous
Whilst the government continues
To carry out arrangements
And arranges
To place the black race
And its environment
Under assignment
To lose its spiritual alignment
By means of mental confinement
It's immorality in its totality
Many casualties will follow
As a result of this reality
As religion
And television
Continues to cause a collision

In the making of decisions
In the minds of men
About how they should be living
They become confused
Unattached
And disassociated
From their true use
And purpose
They're looking to hurt us
Without us even knowing
We've been fooled
Mind control
Is a very powerful tool
They never taught us about
In school
And they're still saying
God save the Queen
But it's God save the little children
Because if it ain't drugs and prison
Then somebody kills them
Now that's realism
But who really listens
The fact is
We face the hardest decisions
If we're to stay living
Overcoming the oblivion

Existing
Within this
Subliminal
And psychological warfare
It's a battle
For the black mind and soul here
So be prepared
Take care
And stay aware.

NO MONEY

A drunken man
Stumbles over to me
From across the street
Begging for change
Saying he's hungry
And wants something to eat
But me
All I've got is my last 50p
No nest eggs
No lump sums
Because insufficient funds
Won't let me be
My money never lasts
Only the memory
Of when I could save
Without hurry
Spend without worry
Money without end
Now I'm at my end
Without money
And I am trying to explain this
To the drunken man
But he won't listen to me
I'm trying to get him to see

That I am in the same position
As he.

OCEAN OF MAGIC POTION

Yesterday
I drank till I was drunk
From an ocean
Of magic potion
That poured into me
And filled me with the notion
Needed for me
To be reassured
And to see once more
That these words
Bleed nothing
But what we need to receive
And I will take it upon me
To repeat every one
Until they're heard
And believed
Learned
And decreed
From out of the mouth
Of numerous nations
Taking heed
To a new breed of conversation
Sparking a renewed vibration
A new league of occupation

Causing a global elevation
The ignoble mind
Can't control
Or conceive the power
Within this emerging generation
Can't see the capability
Behind words and their penetration
Won't see
That we won't be
Until we speak in unity
And formation
You see
We believe in this type of information
And came to hype the occasion
For the writers of a new creed
And nature of persuasion
Persuading them to keep on chasing
And pursuing
To keep on keeping on
Doing what they're doing
Because we need this
We need this
Like flowers need the rain
We need this
Like oxygen needs to reach the brain
We need this

Like those
Who are shackled by their woes
And need to be freed from their pain
We need this
Like those souls
Blowing aimless on the wind of life
Need to find an aim
We need this
Because without this
There's little hope
For even a glimpse of change
Because without this
Everything
Would simply remain the same
And then all that was said
By those gone before
Would have been lost
And said in vain
No more
Shall I bear the strain
Of holding my tongue
No longer
Shall I hold back the emotion
No longer shall I be afraid
To shout out
And express with devotion

That which I deeply feel
Come take a sip
Of a potion that really heals
Come
Come and release and unleash
Those inner voices
Come and see the ocean
Of dreams and multiple choices
Come
Come let us drink
And get drunk together
Come let us drink
And get drunk forever
From an ocean
Of magic potion.

POEM ON THE UNDERGROUND

Ever been on the tube?
I bet you have
Seen all the strange faces
From different places
It's mad
And in the rush hour
Down comes the shower
Of people pushing
And shoving
Pushing
And shoving
Pushing
And shoving
There's a train coming
And a man with a briefcase running
And a woman
With a pram she could fit three sons in
Tell me how the hell
She's going to get that one in

Ever been on the tube?
I have
And the people are so rude
And the lady with her handbag

Won't move
So people can get through
And the man with the dog
That keeps licking people's shoes
Wants a seat for his dog too?
No way
Surely
I should think not
And how can she wear such nice sandals
With pink socks
Damn
Hammersmith and City line
Is chock-a-block
For Highbury, change at King's Cross
Take the Victoria line, and it's one stop
Better swap
If I ever want to make it to West Ham
I'm running late
Will they wait?
Damn
This is not at all what I planned
Held up in a queue
By some slow coach ticket man
And great
Now the escalator's not working
Under repair

Can't they ever get these things fixed
When I'm not here
Attention, this train has a defect
And will be terminating at Euston Square
Will I ever get there this year?

Never been on the tube?
I envy you
Because there's nothing exciting
About standing in a ticket queue
Unless you've got friends with you
But to me that would be very rarely
And highly unlikely most of the time
Especially when they're in bed sleeping
And you've got to be at work
For half nine
After battling your way through
The hell zones of the tube lines
I'm absolutely certain
That like me you'll find
If you survive
That you should have called in sick
Or learnt to drive.

REMEMBER YOU, REMEMBER ME

Remember you
Remember me
We used to share the same energy
Vibrate off of the same frequencies
Our self conduct was nothing but decency
We used to be care free from material wear
We were so in tune with our humanity
Didn't know vanity
We moved more mentally
Than mechanically
Remember you
Remember me
How we used to walk
Across the blue sea effortlessly
How you would talk to me
And I would talk to you
Through telepathy
We were so free
Didn't need weed
Or Hennessy
To get high
Or to get by
We were so in sync
With our own minds

That we could even fly
Remember those times
Picked our own grapes
From our own vines
And boy
Did we make some fine wines
And do I need remind you
Of when we sat around the fire
And intertwined rhymes too
Until it was time to retire
How we clapped our hands
And clicked our fingers
And stamped our feet
To the same drumbeat
How you would run
And I would count
And you would hide
And I would seek
That was our game
Nothing really changed
Except now
They play it in the physical
We used to play it in the brain
Remember
How we used to read the stars
And the constellations

And how we didn't have to visit bars
To get good conversation
Or smoke their cigarettes
How dare we forget
Shame on you
Shame on me
Look at us
With their stuff
We're even wearing their clothes
Don't you know
We wore the finest robes
Whilst sat on the highest thrones
Didn't worship material things though
No mobile phones
On our long distance trips
But still we were equipped
To phone home
Remember me
Remember you
Growing our own food
So plentiful
Going to the same school
Our parents were the teachers
We lived by the same rules
No religious preachers

To keep us fooled
So high in our spirituality
We had one to ones too
With our creators
And that was cool
Remember those times
When fruit and water
Was just enough
Used to live in our heads then
Not in our guts
Yeah
That was us
Vibing off of each others intellect
See
No BBC
No Sky Digital
No TV
So how could you neglect me
Or me neglect you
I was your entertainment
You were mine
I had to respect you
Trying to get through
Trying to get you to see
The bigger picture
How it was

Now we're out
In the wilderness
Can't remember
Where we lived
We must be lost
It's true
We must because
You can't remember me
And I can only just
Remember you.

SENDING OUT AN SOS

Recently
To me
These days seem
Like all I need
Is to get away
Like my life is a mess
And the fight to help myself
Just seems so helpless
Like all I can do
Is send out an SOS
And hope for something
Or someone to come
And end my distress
Like I'm in stormy winds
In a sinking ship
With the cold ocean
Beating against my chest
Like steel cord
With no life preserver
To preserve my life
If I should get tossed overboard
I'm lost in the sea of no hope
And what's more
I can't see the lord

I feel so forsaken and forlorn
Sometimes I wish I was never born
My heart hurts so much these days
I think a piece is torn
Or was soaked in honey
And then left for bees to swarm
But nevertheless
Unlike that Candyman
I seek no revenge
I just sit away alone in my room
And contemplate my end
Because throughout my life
I have cried so many nights
And considered suicide
Again and again
And sometimes in my mind
My death means more than my life
Because I just ain't got those kind of friends
I mean
It seems hopeless
Like mostly everybody
Just wants to take away from me
And when I ain't got what they want
They just want to break away from me
Maybe when I'm gone
They'll just want me

But honestly
That I don't see
Because it's all for one
And one for all now
Meaning
He's turned tough
And wants all the cake in town
And these days
They just don't make enough to go around
So to call these people friends
Is like taking two steps up
To fall six steps down
Because when I'm lost
So-called friends
Just can't be found
On whom can I depend
When I'm down and out
Perhaps I've just misunderstood
What friendships are about
I wonder could I just stop
And end this now
By separating myself from people
And my surroundings for a while
I can't breathe
And I can't think
And I can't smile

I'm under pressure
And I'm in panic
I see danger up ahead
I'm in a sinking ship
And titanics
And icebergs
Just don't mix
I feel all choked again
Like anxiety
Is gripping at my throat again
I feel like I can't cope again
I feel like I'm floating
In that lifeboat of no hope again
I feel like I'm at the end of my rope again
And that's why recently
To me
These days seem
Like all I need
Is to get away
Like all I need
Is to get away
Like all I need
Is to get away
Like all I need
Is to get away
Like all I need

Is to get
A
Way.

SEVENTH HEAVEN

Welcome
So glad you could make it
We've been expecting you
For a while now
We knew you were coming
We just didn't know when
Or how
As you'll see
Things run very different here
This was your way
Before you became unaware
You were seduced
Into all the wrong ways
And led down a crooked path
That once was straight
So glad you could make it
Before it became too late
Here you will find the truth
That has been kept a secret
Here you will find
What you've been searching for
This is where we keep it

Welcome

To the final state
Of eternal bliss
The highest state
Of supreme happiness
Welcome
To the seventh heaven

This is a place
Where there are no wars
And murders are unheard of
Here no one is covetous
No one steals or robs
There is no enviousness
And jealousy just doesn't exist
Here we only focus on necessity
All unnecessaries
Are dismissed
Material possessions
Have little value here
And come secondary
To the preservation of the soul
Maintenance
And preservation of life
Is our primary goal
Here the people smile
And it's always

Always
Good weather
Here we don't drive fancy cars
But we live forever

Welcome
To the final state
Of eternal bliss
The highest state
Of supreme happiness
Welcome
To the seventh heaven

We've prepared a place for you
Hoping you'll stay
Because you'll be safe here
But you can always leave
Anytime you want
If you should ever wish
To go back there
Take a look around you
Take a good look
What do you see?
Yes
These are real people
Living together

In peace
And harmony
You see
We have only one religion here
It's called truth
And honesty
Here we understand
Our purpose for being
And have made it our number one
Policy
And priority
So glad you could make it
Some have been
Led down the crooked path
So far
Their steps are hard to retrace
It's only a very few people
Who ever find this place

Welcome
Once again
To the final state
Of eternal bliss
The highest state
Of supreme happiness
Once again

I say welcome
To the seventh heaven.

SHE DANCES

There was even
Something in the way
She entered the room
Afterwards
You see
Previously
She had been there
That night
On the floor
And it was like
You could feel it
Any night
You walked in the place
She was there
You could be sure
The rhythms of her hips
Still clung to the walls
Of men's psyche
As the condensation
That lent itself
Ever so politely
To the ceiling
Dripped in her name
They both came there

Nightly
She came because
She had made it her job
And because it would mean
Less cash flow
In her bank balance if she stopped
They came there
For what they really wish
They had at home
And really should've had
But never got
She definitely
Had something to offer though
It was in her timing
It was in her rhythm
It was in her expression
It was in her flow
She hypnotised men
With the way she danced
The way she moved
Would put you in a trance
At one glance
No man or even woman
Could be held accountable
For taking their chance
For she was incredibly beautiful

And dynamic
She was a people magnet
And if there was any way
Any woman
Ever desired to be physically
Then she had it
And they wanted to grab it
But they just couldn't have it
Because she had it
In such a way
That they could only go
With the flow of her habit
Under the control
Of her spell
Like magic
And when on her planet
Everything
Just seems to slow down
Almost to the point
Where everything stops
And you could hear
A pin drop
Though the heavy bass line
From the speakers
Still rocks
And there's over a dozen people

Yelling at bar staff
Wondering why other people
Coming to the bar after them
Are being served
And they're not
And another two hundred
Are on the dance floor
Making even more noise
Because it's a bank holiday
And they haven't got work at 9 o'clock
And even though the MC
Just asked who wants more Soca
After the Hip-hop
And there's about fifty people
With whistles and horns
Giving it everything they've got
You could still hear
A pin drop
Because she was hot
And mesmerising
And when you were in her zone
You were alone
Couldn't hear or say a thing
You just had to watch her body sing
And glow
Like a sodium lamp

Watch her go
She's the podium champ
And though her clothes were damp
She followed the code of a vamp
Cunningly seductive
And it worked
She was hired
To keep the club on fire
And it worked
She was finally being paid
For something she loved to do all day
Anyway
So she worked
And played
At the same time
Until it was time to go backstage
And change
And all she's thinking about
Is counting out her change
To see how much money she's made
On top of her minimum wage
Thinking how much time
She would've saved
If she had utilised her talents
At an earlier age
But like most of us

She was challenged
By those rainy days
Now she just works and plays
As she dances her pains away
While men just watch and pay
As she takes their brains away
Like slaves
As they gaze at her with praise
And another of her days
Has just come to an end
But she will be here
Tomorrow
At the same time
Again.

SILENT CHEERLEADERS

Tormenting you with a presence
That only you can see
Cheerleaders who exist in silence
Cheerleaders who are never heard
Cheerleaders that nobody knows exist
Supporters lurking in the shadows
Applauding you where it's unseen
Secret handshakes and high fives
Your silent cheerleaders only torment
Many talkers who say nothing
Preachers who preach in public
Praise you only in private
People say talk is cheap
Here it's worth too much
Many tormented by the silence
Still they do not speak.

TALKING ABOUT YOU AND ME

These streets got me going crazy
Don't know who to trust
Everybody's shady
Because there's all kinds of people
And there's all kinds of hell
But we've got to stick to our plans
We can't afford to fail
We can't be moved
By the negative that surrounds
We've got to keep on rising
Onto higher ground
Some say who are we
To be bearers of the light
But I say
Who are we not to be
We've got to be
Time goes
So slowly sometimes
When we can't get through
It seems
Like we're just a lonely few
Chasing a dream
But I've got to keep my head up

Just as much as I can
Got to keep on moving
Like a homeless man
Though it seems some people
Only want to see you down
And they're only happy
When you're not around
We can't be bound
By those devils of yesterday
We can't be bound
By those who've been led astray
Some say
Good things come to those who wait
But I really don't know about that
Because I don't choose to hesitate

I'm talking about you and me
Talking about ways we need to be
I'm talking about me and you
Talking about things we're going through
I'm talking about you and me
Talking about the way it's got to be
I'm talking about me and you
Talking about things we need to do

My brother told me

How to do the thing right
He said, keep the faith
And don't give up the fight
Because only you will know
When it's good to go
Don't turn around
Because they told you so
And don't be afraid
To speak on how you feel
If you don't like it
Let them know the deal
Because those hidden emotions
Will do you no right
And they eventually
Will hurt you inside
I can see them down yonder
Watching me
They've got plans
For what they want me to be
But I've got to keep my head up
Just as much as I can
Because now that we've started
How can we turn around
When all we've been searching for
Will soon be found
Come on, come on

We haven't got much time
Better read the signs
So we can do what's right
To free our minds
Before the coming of the daylight
It won't be long
Until we never need
A redemption song
To set our minds at ease
We'll all be free

I'm talking about you and me
Talking about ways we need to be
I'm talking about me and you
Talking about things we're going through
I'm talking about you and me
Talking about the way it's got to be
I'm talking about me and you
Talking about things we need to do.

THE A.R.T.I.S.T

He always
Says a few short mantras
In the form of a quiet prayer
To himself
As he carefully selects
And lays out
His choice of brushes
And colours
He would be using
For that particular day

He would say
There's a certain
Creative doorway
You must mentally
Pass through
Before you can ever
Even have a hope
In making love
To the canvas

You see
It was his belief
That each new canvas

Should be treated
Like a beautiful woman
You were being intimate with
For the first time
The same care
With which she would be touched
Is the same care
With which you should use the brush
From beginning
To end
From the very first time you approached
Until the moment you departed

He said
Each and every stroke
Should be exact
Precise
And accounted for
By the artist
Nothing should be
Accidental
Or without reason
The artist must
Understand
And be in tune with
The principles

Governing the higher self
Allowing him to account
For all he produces
Both in the conscious mind
And in the subconscious

He often spoke of karmic law
Applying it in the idea
That the canvas
Could only be a reflection
Of what the painter
Had initially put into it
Hence
He never failed
To stress the importance
Of preparation
And forming the right energy
Within the space
In which you were going to work
For this reason
He had designed his easel
So that it could safely hold a candle
Burning at both sides

He said
For him

124

The presence of them
Added something
To his environment
And his creative spirit

He said
But each painter
Has his own thing
Whether it's candles
The smell of incense
A particular type of lighting
Music
Even food
Whatever
But he will have something
Even if the painter
Doesn't realise it himself consciously
There will always
Be something used
To enhance mood
Even if involuntary
But the key to mastery
Is being aware of the affects
Of their presence
And to then
Choose appropriately

According to
What you were aiming to achieve
For that particular painting

He never kept the subjects
Of painting
And the mind
Far apart
He often talked about
The importance
Of developing
A photographic memory
He said
The painter must become
Like a sponge
Absorbing all that he sees
Soaking up the entirety
Of the atmosphere
That surrounds him
Both indoors and out

And on the subject of versatility
He would say
The artist must master
How to alter and shift
From a blissful state of mind

To a despondent state of mind
At the blink of an eye
He said this is necessary
In terms of the artist
Reaching different extremes
Within his art

He would say
The artist must learn
How to make triple M's
Out of double M's
Meaning
The artist must
Learn how to make
Magnificently mellow moments
Out of melancholy moods
And vice versa
Even if he doesn't feel that way
He must create it
Because it's the result he wants
Which are the thoughts
And the emotions
That are stirred
In all
That see
His work.

THE GAME OF LIFE

Now tell me
Where do we go from here
A place where another day
Is another year
Because time just flies by so fast
Before you know it
Another week has passed
With another unfinished task
And more bills to pay
With money that never lasts
It seems so unfair
And I swear
It's as though no one hears
Or cares
As long as they get theirs
The ways of this world
Brings tears
And some
Have even given up their dreams too
It seems cruel
That for the next man to make it
He's got to take it from you
But what can you do
It's either 1. You quit the game

Or 2. You push on through
Now between me and you
Quitters never win a thing
Or do the do
So I'd go for No. 2
And pray that it's enough
To survive
The tough lifestyle of the city
The hustle and bustle
Has got everybody looking tired
And it's a pity
We have to work so hard
Just to eat
Just to stay on our feet
And make ends meet
Not to mention
Deal with the oppression
In the street
Sometimes I wonder
How we compete
And still stay complete
In this game of life
That's so hard to play
And so hard to beat
But nevertheless
Deal me in

Because there's no way
I'll ever win
Sitting on the sideline
It's a waste of time
And the best way
To make sure I never shine
So give me a place in the race
And I'll be there
At the finish line
Why
Because in this game
There's no second try
The game of life, baby
The game
Of
Life.

THE GREAT CREATORS

Tell yourself
You are worthy
Of everything you desire in life
Tell yourself
You are deserving
Of all the good
That this world has to give
Claim your place
Among those who have decided
They have found their great calling
And pursue just that
Those who honour their dreams
And visions
Who see the unseen
And hear the unheard
And say the unsaid
Who take something from nothing
And create that which never was
Those who struggle and toil
For their ambition
Who define their goal
And focus their aim there
Who do not give in
Who do more

Who do more than that
Who tell themselves
Yes
Those who quest for success
In spite of the rest
Those who expect it
And will accept nothing less
Those who don't let doubt deny them
Those who enjoy making use
Of the shade
And the shadows
Those who delay gratification
And endure pain
Those who sacrifice
Small short-term immediate pleasures
For greater gain
In deeper
More meaningful
Longer lasting fulfilment
Those triers who never tire
Those inspired
And on fire
Those who don't let the opinions
Of others define them
Those who sculpt their future
From the invisible

Who shape things
From the intangible
Those who paint the definitions
And create the meanings
Those who walk tall
And faithfully
Knowing they have the ability
To affect their trajectory
At any moment
And in any direction they choose
The power to manifest
That which isn't
Or never was
The capacity to invent
Reinvent
Transform
And change things
Everything
Including themselves.

THE SHAKE UP

Bro
Personally
I couldn't care less
How much your Timberland boots cost
But where I come from
The boys will be glad to see you
And quick to help you take them off
Along with your flashy Avirex leather
They'll stick a knife to your neck
And strip you out of it
Just for pleasure
And you're still thinking you're hot
But that might change
When you find yourself
Trying to get home
In the freezing cold
In just your vest and your socks
And who you going to call
With no phone and no money
You'll be another black man
In Hackney
With no shoes
Begging for change for the phone box
That's funny

You might have a long wait, bruv
First thing people are going to think
Is that you want it for drugs
Don't play
You hear a couple of 2Pac songs
Smoke some weed
And you feel you're a thug
No way
Know your place
You better find a smile
Somewhere under that screw face
You might think you're Ready to Die
Until you get on the wrong side
Of a guy
Who is ready to oblige
And when you feel that knife
Against your side
You will apologise
And with that gun to your head
You will take back what you said
So have some respect
And watch where you step
And where you go
Because this ain't no film set
Or music video
This is where the drama really happens

Where you can hear guns clapping
Over bad drug deals
Where the police are in on it too
And kids might shoot you
Just to see how it feels
Bro, this is real
And nobody here even bothers to ask
Where's the love now
When 14 year olds
Are wearing bullet proof vests
To the club now
The same club
Across the road
From where you're likely to knifed
For trying to break up that fight
Yeah
The same club
They brought out the riot police for
The other night
Which is just around the corner
From a police shoot out
A hostage situation
And a fifteen day siege
And if you're coming in peace
Then you're hanging in the wrong place
Because here

It's long face to long face
Prison time and court dates
Bloodstained concrete
Flowers
Funerals
And more police tape
Day and night
The street music is sirens
Just keeping you alert
And awake
Emergency services
That don't seem to be saving a life
Clearly
Drug and gun crime initiatives
Aren't working right
Because too many boys like you
Are still dying
From the effects of both
And, bro
I can see you now
On your side
On the cold pavement
Blood pouring out of your mouth
Holding your stomach
Holding your other hand out
To a passing blue Tigra

And red Nissan for help
Heaving from the pain
And your hands
Both your hands
Are covered in blood
And your white Nike vest
Soaked
It's cold
It's so cold
And the ambulance
Is taking so long
And then I wake up
Always at that point
Still hearing the sounds in my head
But this ain't no dream
In fact
The one who should really wake up here
Is you
Open your eyes
Read your local paper
Watch the news
Why do you think
They call here Murder mile
Because, bro
This ain't no film set
Or music video

This is where the drama really happens
Where you can hear guns clapping
Over bad drug deals
Where the police are in on it too
And kids might shoot you
Just to see how it feels
Bro, this
Is real.

THE STRUGGLES WE OVERCOME

Your life isn't shaped
By your experiences
But by the stories
You tell yourself
About what they mean
Pictured here
With all my past failures
Insecurities
Losses
Disappointments
Fears
Regrets
Doubts
Successes
Strengths
Triumphs
Satisfaction
Happiness
Courage
Certainty
Dreams
Hopes
And passion for the future
I've learned that change

Actually happens in an instant
It's the making the decision
And the getting ready
To change
That can take a second
A day
Or a lifetime
How long it takes
To make that change
Is up to you
It can happen in a moment
Sometimes what you don't do
Is more powerful
Than what you do
There's something to learn
From everyone's story
And the story
Is only just beginning
We are a product
Of the sacrifices we make
The pain we endure
The struggles
We overcome.

THESE WORDS

Let these words
Eternally bless you
As they
Undress
And caress you
Stroke you
And provoke you
Open you
And evoke in you
A desire
Wild as fire
A need
Irreplaceable
A passion
Aggressive
And insatiable
A lust
For loose lips
That drip
Words
In multiples
So freely
So frequent
And so hot

That you won't want them
To stop
Running
But keep coming
And coming
And coming

Let these words
Get in you
Touch every nerve
And sinew
Let them send you
Hurled into
Worlds renewed
Serve you with a verse
From the food of truth
Shelter and clothe you
Wash over you
Clean you
Redeem you
Take you deep within
Parts of yourself
You've never been to
Thought you might never find
Never see
Or in your lifetime

Get to go to
In their embrace
Let them enfold you
Hold you
Mould you
And control you
Let them forever
Remind your spirit
Mind
Body
And soul
From head to toe
That I
Phenzwaan
Told you

To be
Reassured
And to make no mistake
That you can respect
And take these words
Or you can reject
And hate these words
But you will never ever
Be able to forget
Or forsake these words

Neglect
Or shake these words
Dissect
Or break these words
Are
Composed in phonetic code
Not verse
So
Such attempts
Would only serve
To recreate these words
Even now
As I speak
They seep deep
Into your subconscious
Changing from form to form
Like the universe
Is vast
Are free

Free as the unseen seed
That freely grows
Free as the unseen energy
That freely flows
Free as the very breath
Flowing from your nose

Free as the unseen force
Of spiritual law that controls
Let them steal you
Let them heal you
Let them elevate your soul
These words of sustenance
Penned for empty bowls
Let them fill you up
Warm you up
Give you goose bumps
Curl your toes
Let them itch you
Let them scratch you
Annoy you
Get all up in your clothes
Let them course right through your veins
Like our ancestor's woes

Let them in
Let them under your skin
Into your flesh
Into your bones
Let them get to you
Let them infect you
Let them kill you
Resurrect

And rebuild you
These words used to raise slaves
From the dead
And they still do
Let them will you
Fulfil you
Distil you
Thrill you
Chill you
In the blistering cold
Of their winter nights
Singe you
In the hot heat
Of their blazing sunlight
Because
You see
I want you to feel these words
Digest these words
Deep inside your chest
Conceal these words
Breathe these words
As I speak these words
Be replete with these words
So even in sleep
You can repeat these words
I believe every soul

Across the globe
Should know these words
So I go tell these words
Go sell these words
Go through
And repel hell with these words
And here now
They dwell
Like the tenacious scent
Of nature's purest herbs
Can you smell these words
Can you
Permeating
Like the sweet fragrance
From Egyptian oils
Pressed from precious flowers
Cultivated on Egyptian soil
Just lingering
Dip your fingers in
And hold these words
Never let go of these words
Always uphold these words
Never shun these words
Or run from these words

Instead...

Chase these words
Come face these words
Come taste these words
Grafted from
Years of tears and pain
Crafted on behalf of the slain
And all those still here
In this struggle to maintain
And as many walk these cold streets
Begging for change
When will enough people see
That they're not really
Begging for change
They are begging
For
Change
And who knows
They may too claim me insane
Because I'm here right now
Doing the same
So come take these words
Before it's too late for words
Assimilate these words
Appreciate these words
Articulate these words
Perpetuate these words

And if the day should come
When men aim
To tame these words
Shame these words
Change
Rearrange
Restrain
Or set up against these words
My friend
Until the end
Defend these words
And when my physical
Can no longer contain
Comprehend
Explain
Or ascend these words
Remember these words
These lyrics
Etched into the very depths
Of your spirit
Forever living
Left where you'll never forget
They exist
Where you can never resist
Their rhythm
Hauntingly beautiful

They will be heard
Until then
I'll keep giving
And giving
And giving
And giving
And giving
And giving
These
Words.

TOO SOON

Post-war
Brutalist
Architecture housing
19th floor
Up above
Everything surrounding
Lift smells like piss
When it's operational
Asbestos walls
Cockroaches in the hall
Shitty pigeons decorate the balcony
Inner city living ain't great
That's just a fallacy
I heard a kid killed another kid
Over a cigarette
Went to prison
And not a word told in the Gazette
One summer time
A big television station
Came and filmed us all
Living in degradation
Just to play it all on our TVs
For entertainment
Old metal electric meter

Only took 50 pence pieces
To keep the power on
That's all the household needed
Lived just a stone throw away
From the primary school gate
Couldn't wait to go home
And play all my favourite tapes
Rode around the estate
On bicycle cruises
Became a champion
Of scrapes
And skateboard bruises
Along with
All of the other young winners
And sore losers
Ball games against the wall
And new friends
Who then only knew
Barbie dolls
And action men
Wild girls
And naughty boys
Grew up fast
And sought other toys
Newsagents
Located just at the bottom of the road

Sold Space Raiders
Stickers
Penny sweets
And Beanos
Who knew
Just what life would've been
When copies of Just Seventeen
Was my favourite magazine
I liked the pop stars and the pop charts
Song lyrics
And pin-up posters
I'd pin up in my room
Before long
It was all over
And we grew up too soon.

UNWELCOME

Metaphorically speaking
I thought I was a guest here
I thought I was welcome
In this house
I thought I was allowed
To sleep on this couch
Now you are telling me
To keep my mouth
Not to speak out
Just to leave this house
At once
And to go back
Where I came from
I came here because
I was lead to believe
I would be well received
Well appreciated
And well treated
Well accepted
And well respected
Irrespective
Of my cultural perspective
But I was wrong
I was wrong

I was wrong
Your face was smiling
But what you were really saying
Is that you are going to close your eyes
And count to five
And when you open them
I'd better be gone
Or else
I never did feel at home
Taking food from your shelf
Even though you said
I could always help myself
It seemed like a crime
Every time
Like I was taking something
That wasn't mine
That's how it felt
And that the more I took
The more I would be forever
Indebted to you
Through accepting your handouts
Which you would one day
Rewind
And remind me of
So I never forget it
And look now

It's true
And somehow
I am supposed to show you gratitude
But all I can do
Is show you attitude
Because in my view
I've been confused
Used
Abused
And refused
But I refuse
To be confused
Used
Abused
And refused anymore
So I am leaving
Metaphorically speaking.

VICTORY IS YOURS

Take your positions, men
You are the new platoon now
You will take up the banner
Of those gone before
You will be the upholders
Of our divisional territory
You will fight
For first place on the outfield
Don't run from it
Embrace it
It's yours
What are you running for
It's only when you stop running
From your responsibility
As soldiers
In this more so mental war
Than anything else
And stand up and fight for it
Because you owe it to yourself
That you're going to see any benefits
That you're going to see any changes
Because it won't be handed to you
Oh no
That's for sure

It's only when you learn
To control your circumstances
And not have them control you
It's only when you can think
95% solution
And 5% problem
It's only when you do these things
It's only when you can stand guard
At the door of your mind
It's only then
That you're going to reap the rewards
Of true warriors
Fighting without relent
To obtain their God given birthright
It's a struggle
Believe it's a struggle
It's a hell of a struggle
But let me tell you
No battalion
Ever wins a battle butter smooth
Oh no
It's going to be rough
It's got to be rough
Oh yeah
Because it's only through the harshness
Of the experience

That you're going to realise
That the very thing
You fought for
Down in the valley
Is what you're going to celebrate
On the mountain top
If you stick it out
It's only through the harshness
Of the experience
That you're going to be able to
Have a true appreciation
And understanding
Of what the victory means
And why
You fought so hard to get it
If you stick it out
That's why
That's why you've got to face it full on
Not run
Because when you stop running
You realise
You're still unfulfilled
Still incomplete
Still lost
Still searching
And then it hits you

All at once
There's a reason
Why you needed to fight
There's something you wanted
There's a goal
You were trying to achieve
You've run away
And now you're further away
From winning
And overcoming
And obtaining that goal
Than when you started
You're in a circle
And it's only when
You decide to make an attempt
To break out of that circle
Meaning
Stand up and fight
And stop running
It's only then
That you're going to see results
It's only then
That triumph will be yours
It's only then
That you break out
Of that attempting and failing

Attempting and failing
Repetitive circle
That's cordoned you off in the past
From achieving what you really want
It's only then
That you're going to feel complete
It's only then
You're going to feel fulfilled
The outcome of this conflict
Is in your hands
So take your positions, men
You are the new platoon now
You will take up the banner
Of those gone before
You will be the upholders
Of our divisional territory
You will fight
For first place on the outfield
Don't run from it
Embrace it
Because it's yours.

WHAT'S UP, SMOKEY?

What's up, Smokey
Nicotine throaty
Buy a pack of fags at the bar
Hope you got iron lungs
Gonna' need a couple, son
If you're gonna' swallow all that tar
I know you like B&H
To make you die an early age
Bet you left a packet in the car
Heard your dad likes Hamlet
Hope his throat can handle it
Think it was either that
Or Panama cigars
I know your girl likes Silk Cut
Seen her smoke them to the butt
Trying to cut her little life in half
Said she loves to smoke a cancer stick
Keeps her slim won't keep her fit
Your girl, you know
She really makes me laugh
And what's up with marijuana chest
Still wanna' have a little test
To find out which one-ah smokes da' best
Mix a little weed in

The one without the seeds in
And let lung cancer do the rest
He used to smoke like a chimney
Oh I didn't know
Forgive me
I bet now he wishes he didn't even start
Please send him my regards
Dealing with emphysema
Must be really hard
And I'm really sorry
To hear that thing about his heart

So long, Smokey
Nicotine throaty
Buy another pack of fags at the bar
Hope you got iron lungs
Gonna' need a couple, son
If you're gonna' swallow all that tar
I always knew you liked B&H
To make you die an early age
But I didn't know you'd find an early grave.

WHEN THE WRITING STOPS

When the writing stops
They say they have writer's block
But writer's block doesn't exist
Writer's block never did
Resurrecting an old myth
A thing that never lived
This scapegoat for their sin
That the gods find no pleasure in

When the writing stops
They think it is writer's block
But those who can write, write
And know that it is not

When the writing stops
You proclaim it's writer's block
While the writers carry on
And when we pause to ask where
Is your illusive muse now
You still tell us of a unicorn
Kidnapped
And held in bondage
By a ghost
That cannot write.

WHO AM I?

Take a listen
And a deep look
In my eyes
I am
The fisher of men
That those men
Despise
That night
When the tortured
And tormented
Cried out
In the moonlight
I am the one who
Heard their cries
I am their
Ever permeating
Presence
Their effervescence
Their everlasting
Essence
I am your
Soul provider
Your soul reviver
Because souls

Have become
Old
And tired
Cold
And uninspired
I am that vessel
And you shall
Respect me
Because I am
Of the one
That reflects the moon
And shines the sun.

ABOUT THE AUTHOR

Phoenix James is an award winning Writer, Poet, Author and Spoken Word Recording Artist. He began performing his poetic words live on stages across the UK in 1998. His debut spoken word poetry album, *The A.R.T.I.S.T,* was released in 2000. His first limited edition printed collection of poetry, *To Whom It May Concern,* was published in 2003. He has toured and performed his poetry internationally since 2004. He has appeared in films, on television and radio shows, and collaborated with other artists, singer-songwriters, actors, musicians, filmmakers and producers. In 2013, he wrote, directed and produced the feature length mock documentary film, *Love Freely but Pay for Sex.* Phoenix James has written, recorded and released several spoken word poetry albums including, *Phenzwaan Now & Forever* (2009), *A Patchwork Remedy for A Broken Melody* (2020), *FREE* (2021), *Haven for the Tormented* (2021), *With All That Said* (2022), and *Remixes* Volumes: 1 & 2 (2022).

If you enjoyed reading this book, please leave a review online. The author reads every review and they help new readers discover his work.

PHOENIX JAMES

Photo by Phoenix James

Phoenix James lives in London, England.

Connect with Phoenix James on his online social media platforms via www.linktr.ee/ Phoenix_James and say you've read this book. To contact or learn more about Phoenix James and his creative journey or to receive updates via his Newsletter Mailing List, visit his official website at www.PhoenixJamesOfficial.com

Phoenix James Official